PALM PAINTING C

MW01079547

Are you ready to spark your child's imagination with Palm Painting fun? This book is filled with prompts to get you talking, moving, and creating with your child.

Why is this book important?

The Clever Hands series features a lesson on every spread, so you have everything you need to create a dynamic art class at home. Created by experts Olga Uzorova and Elena Nefedova, this proven educational methodology develops speech and fine motor skills through one of the most creative and entertaining activities: finger painting! This unique approach to childhood development includes clear, interactive instructions designed to spark conversation while boosting self-assuredness and imagination. Moreover, the techniques promote one-on-one communication between you and your child, ensuring the time spent together is valuable and fun.

So, grab some paint, and get started creating masterpieces and memories!

How does it work?

1) Start by looking at the completed palm art illustration on the left-hand page of each example. Then ask the questions marked with this symbol ⊚.

2) Next, enhance learning through movement by doing the activities marked with this symbol ⊚.

3) Now look at the incomplete illustration on the right-hand page. Review the directions and explain them to your child BEFORE they dip into the paint. Rotate the book to help with palm placement.

4) Let your child press their palm into the paint and have fun! You may want to use a brush to help spread the paint on their palm more evenly.

5) Celebrate your child's achievement! Let them fill the circle on their painting with the matching sticker when you see this symbol ⊚.

Before you begin...

● Cover the surface you want to paint on with newspaper or a tarp.

● Set up your paints and water bowl, and keep a brush nearby to help spread paint on palms.

● Wash hands. They should be cleaned before and after you paint.

● Sit next to your child and get started!

A princess wears a crown and a beautiful gown.

◎ Can you point to the princess's crown?
◎ Let's count the dots on her gown.

◎ We can make crowns with our fingers! *(Demonstrate: Fan out the fingers of one hand and let them peek out above the back of your head.)*

◎ Place the golden crown sticker on the circle.

Dip palm and fingers in YELLOW paint. Spread fingers and press down above the princess's head to make her crown. Use a fingertip to paint the dots on her dress.

STICKER

The baby chicks  are safe and warm, mama hen protects them from all harm.

◎ Can you point to mama hen's wing?
◎ Mama hen's wing is made of five feathers. Let's count them!

◎ Mama hen cuddles her chicks.
   (Demonstrate: Wrap your arms around yourself or your child in a hug.)

◎ Place the baby chick sticker on the circle.

Dip palm and fingers in ORANGE paint. With fingers together, press palm against mama hen's side. Use a fingertip to paint dots on her chest.

STICKER

Do you see something swish? Must be the tail of a fish !

◎ Point to the fish's tail.

◎ Where are the fish's scales?

◎ Let's pretend we have a tail fin like this fish. Swish, swish. *(Demonstrate: Place palms together with fingers spread out and swish them back and forth).*

◎ Place the little fish sticker on the circle.

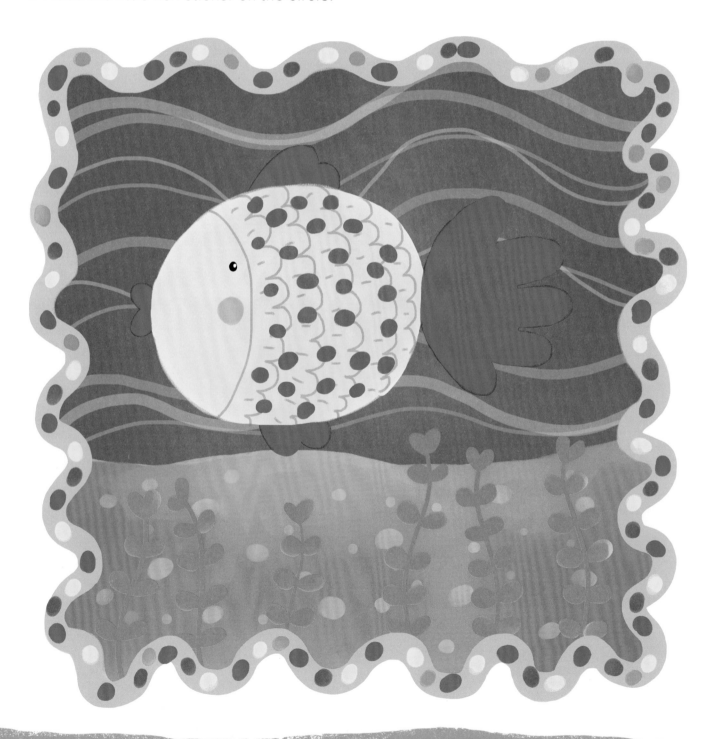

Dip palm and fingers in RED paint. Spread fingers and press down behind the fish to make its tail. Use a fingertip to paint the fish's scales.

I'm an octopus, and it's true, I have a few more arms than you!

◎ Point to the octopus's arms.
◎ An octopus should have 8 legs. Let's count how many this one has!

◎ Let's use 8 of our fingers to make our own octopus legs. *(Demonstrate: Tuck thumbs in. Place hands together with eight fingers pointing out and wiggle them.)*

◎ Place the happy octopus sticker on the circle.

Dip fingers in RED paint. Use the faint image of legs on the picture as a placement guide and press fingers down. Use one finger to add three more legs. Use a fingertip to add dots.

STICKER

Somewhere underneath the sea a jellyfish floats by silently.

◉ Point to the jellyfish's tentacles.
◉ Where is her bell-shaped body?

◉ Let's move our fingers like the jellyfish moves its tentacles!
  (Demonstrate: Pointing the fingers of one hand down, spread all five out wide, then squeeze them back together--and repeat.)

◉ Place the jolly jellyfish sticker on the circle.

Dip palm and fingers in BLUE paint. With fingers spread, press down on the page to make tentacles fanning out beneath the jellyfish's bell-shaped body.

STICKER

Sometimes a dragon  breathes with fire.
A scaly suit is his attire.

◎ Can you point to the dragon's fiery flames?
◎ Point to the scales on the dragon's neck and tail.

◎ Let's pretend that we are a fire-breathing dragon! *(Demonstrate: Take a deep breathe in, open your mouth wide, and blow out the air — just like a dragon!)*

◎ Place the friendly dragon sticker on the circle.

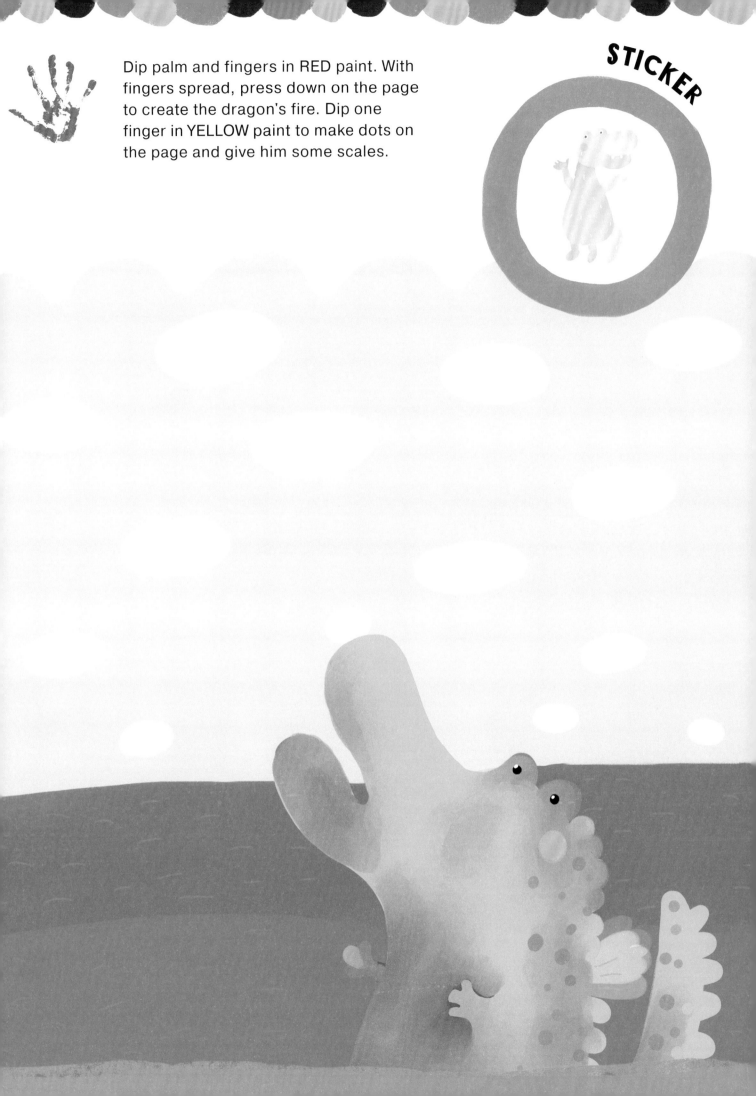

Dip palm and fingers in RED paint. With fingers spread, press down on the page to create the dragon's fire. Dip one finger in YELLOW paint to make dots on the page and give him some scales.

STICKER

"I do not gallop," said the seahorse , "I much prefer to swim, of course".

◎ Show the seahorse's big fin.
◎ Can you point to his tail?

◎ Let's pretend that we are just like a seahorse and nibble on some seaweed!
  (Demonstrate: purse your lips together and then bob your head.)

◎ Place the fancy seahorse sticker on the circle.

Dip your palm and fingers in the YELLOW paint. With fingers spread, press down on the page to give the seahorse a fancy fin.

STICKER

The daffodils  are opening,
telling me it's almost spring.

◎ Point at the yellow crown of the flower.
◎ A flower has beautiful petals. Let's count them!

◎ Imagine that you are picking a pretty daffodil bouquet with your child. *(Demonstrate: open and close your pointer and middle to imitate the motion of a pair of scissors, as if cutting daffodil stems.)*

◎ Place the pretty daffodil sticker on the circle.

Dip palm and fingers in the YELLOW paint. With fingers together, press down on the page to give the daffodil a delicate crown. Dip one finger in the YELLOW paint and add pebbles. What a beautiful flower!

STICKER

On his head he wears a crown , and there's the throne where he sits down

◎ Point to the king's nose.
◎ The king sits on a grand throne. What color is it?

◎ Let's pretend that we are a king and wearing a crown! *(Demonstrate: stretch your hands and arms above your head. Now, slowly bring them down, as if carefully placing a crown on your head.)*

◎ Place the grand crown sticker on the circle.

Dip your palm and fingers in the RED paint. With fingers spread, press down on the page to make a dazzling crown. Dip one finger in BLACK paint and dot the king's cape.

STICKER

I will plant a healthy carrot to brighten up my summer salad.

◎ Can you point the carrots' green stalks?
◎ Carrots grow from seeds. Count them below!

◎ Let's pretend that we are farmers and picking carrots for our summer salad! *(Demonstrate: use your hands to grasp imaginary carrots in the ground. Now, yank them up!)*

◎ Place the cheerful carrot sticker on the circle.

Dip palm and fingers in GREEN paint. With spread fingers, press down on the page to make the carrots' leaves. Dip one finger in BROWN paint. Dot the page to create carrot seeds.

STICKER

Poppy flowers 🌺, as you see, are as red as red can be!

◎ Point at the petals of the poppy flowers.
◎ Poppies have green stems. Point to them, too!

◎ Let's pretend that we are a bee buzzing around the sweet-smelling poppies.
   (Demonstrate: make a bee's "buzzing" sound. Have your child join you!)

◎ Place the pretty poppy flower sticker on the circle.

Dip your palm and fingers in RED paint. With fingers spread, press down on the page to make pretty poppy flowers.

STICKER

One, two, three. One, two, three! How many palm trees 🌴 can you see?

◎ Show the trunk of the palm tree.
◎ Now, point to the palm tree's leaves.

◎ Let's pretend that we are palm tree, stretching up to the sun! *(Demonstrate: spread your fingers wide and reach your arms above you. Wave your arms as if they are blowing in the breeze. Have your child pretend to be a palm tree too!)*

◎ Place the strong palm tree sticker on the circle.

Dip palm and fingers in the GREEN paint. With fingers spread, press down on the page to make the palm tree's leaves. Dip one finger in the BROWN paint. Create three coconuts just under the leaves.

STICKER

Big trees 🌳 reach up toward the sky. They grow so fast, and so do I.

◎ Can you point to the tree's leaves?

◎ Where is the trunk of the tree?

◎ Let's pretend that we are leaves falling from the tree. *(Demonstrate: With arms and hands reached above your head, spread your fingers. As you wiggle your fingers, slowly bring your hands to the ground. Have your child create falling leaves with their hands, too!)*

◎ Place the leafy tree sticker on the circle.

Dip palms and fingers in GREEN paint. With fingers spread, press down on the page to give the tree a leafy top. Dip one finger in the BROWN paint. Dot the ground to make pebbles.

STICKER

In the woods, a proud moose  said, "Check out these antlers on my head!"

◎ Point to the moose's big antlers.
◎ Can you find the moose's hooves?

◎ Let's pretend that we are a proud moose with marvelous antlers! *(Demonstrate: with fingers spread, place your hands on your head to represent antlers.)*

◎ Place the proud moose sticker on the circle.

Dip your palm and fingers in the ORANGE paint. With fingers spread, press down on the page to give the moose marvelous antlers. Dip one finger in the YELLOW paint to create yellow flowers in the field.

STICKER

From flower to flower she flies by.
Flutter, flutter, butterfly .

◎ Show the butterfly's tiny antennae.
◎ Now, point to her eyes.

◎ Let's pretend that we are a butterfly, opening and closing our pretty wings.
(Demonstrate: with hands facing one another, place your wrists together. Wiggle your fingers in a fluttering motion. Have your child flutter along with you!)

◎ Place the fluttering butterfly sticker on the circle.

Dip palm and fingers in the BLUE paint. With fingers spread, press down on the page to make the butterfly's wings. Dip one finger in the YELLOW paint. Dot the butterfly's wings to give it a pretty pattern.

STICKER

Dip your palm and fingers in the YELLOW paint. With fingers spread, press it on the page to give the peacock a golden tail. Now, do the same with RED and ORANGE paint!

STICKER